THE KEYS
TO CREATE
UNLIMITED
SUCCESS IN
BUSINESS
CAREER AND
LIFE

JOHN KIRK

Author, Speaker and Trainer

www.JohnKirk.ws
www.facebook.com/JohnKirkSBA
Email: johnkirkonline@gmail.com

ISBN-13: 978-1539660774
ISBN-10: 153966077X

DEDICATION

Special thanks to my youngest daughter Natalie Kirk for her patience and assistance in designing and formatting this book. Natalie has saved me weeks in getting this book to market. Without her knowledge I'd be lost. It's very handy to have a daughter with a Degree (soon to be a Masters) in Animation to set me straight.

CONTENTS

INTRODUCTION

The Keys To Create Unlimited Success In Business, Career And Life has been written especially with **YOU** in mind.

It is directed at anyone who has struck an 'obstacle', a 'blockage', a 'challenge' or some sort of 'pain' in their personal or professional life that they are having difficulty overcoming. Could this be you?

Whether you are thinking about switching careers, starting your first business, or if you have been in business for 10 years, this book will help you to come up with new ideas, create new plans, set bigger goals and focus on **working on designing your life, rather than having it directed for you by someone else that you may not necessarily like.**

The Keys will have you thinking clearer about your career, business or direction in life. It will encourage you to view your business or career as an extension of your lifestyle rather than view it as just another job.

How can this be?

This Book contains a simple set of instructions that anyone can follow....but, **it's not for everyone!**

The Keys may be simple to understand but, the Big Question is:

"Will you follow these critical steps and implement them into your life?"

Let's face it, there are thousands of good business and self-development books out there and this is just another one of them. Many people read, learn and absorb, but very few people actually follow through. In fact, less than 10% of people ever implement what they learn from those who have already done what they want to do.

Leaders like Anthony Robbins and T. Harv Ecker speak to tens of thousands of ordinary people each year. Many of them go away with stars in their eyes, But how many of them implement what they just learnt? Sadly, not a lot. Yet many of these "followers" are back again 12 months later to listen to the Guru's words of wisdom.

Why? Who knows? It really is a mystery, but **lack of follow through is the main reason why there are so many failures in career, business and life!**

Really, this book should be called ***"The Five Pillars of Success"*** because The Keys lay the foundations on solid ground. Get these steps right and the foundations will last into the future. Ignore them at your peril.

There is one thing I can guarantee at this point. Learn **The Keys** and implement what you learn in this Book and you will succeed.

Then, just watch your business/career and life change dramatically over the next 12 months.

WARNING: <u>This book is not about some Get Rich Quick Scheme.</u> The methods taught in this book are based on what I have learnt and applied over many years by listening to and watching the Masters at work... and then following their Action Steps.

I have also taught these strategies and techniques to thousands of Small Business Students. All of the methods discussed in this book are proven to work... but only if you do!

The Objective

The objective of this Book is to help you to step back from your Career/Job/Business and to think carefully about your future direction, your goals and what it is that you really want out of life, over the next 12 months. It is all about *'taking control.'*

What is your really heart saying to you? Is it telling you that this is what you truly desire? Or, is it saying, **"Get out of this job NOW".** Perhaps it's telling you that you're in the wrong business or studying for the wrong Degree.

Your job/career/business should be your servant.....not your master. It should exist so you can live life the way you want to. Sadly, for many people, this is often not the case. Staying abreast of new opportunities, marketing and sales trends is vital to your future success in whatever you choose to do.

Taking the time to continually upgrade your skills and knowledge is critical to success these days and, it's ***your success*** we're talking about. Not mine, not someone else's... just yours.

OK, So What's In It For You?

By following **The Keys** you can expect –

☞ to learn more about what is important,

☞ to think clearer,

☞ to plan and strategise,

☞ to look inside yourself to find out what it is that you really desire, and

☞ to effectively implement what you have learned to increase your opportunities, design your life and achieve success.

After reading this book and implementing each of the 5 Keys, you are likely to see things in a different light. Doors that were previously locked will begin to open for you. This is not unusual. If you have not previously taken a detached look at yourself, you may have missed the opportunities and business trends that can present themselves from time to time.

And why is all of this so important?

Opportunities can present themselves daily. Ignoring them, or just not seeing them, can stifle personal and business growth. Failure to recognise opportunities or business trends can cause negativity, kill ambition and, ultimately, put you behind the 8 ball.

Stay in the game. Reading this Book is just the beginning. Watching the trends, implementing the strategies and following a tried and true path **will increase your chances of personal and professional success.**

All the best from,

John Kirk

Author, Speaker and Trainer

THE FIRST KEY
PREPARATION AND PLANNING

Preparing yourself for success in all aspects of life and business includes (but is not restricted to) having an idea, researching the idea and drawing up a flexible, workable Plan A. Please note that there is no limit to age here. No matter whether you are a teenager or a retiree, you can create your own Plan A and make it work for you –

1.   THE IDEA

- Start by asking yourself, "What would I like to do above all else right now?"

- Then ask, "What Would I Love To Do? What really excites me? What will drive me to get up every day to start work? What will keep me going forward during the tough times?"

- Then check to see if your heart is in it. Why? Because your heart dictates your "stickability" and your ultimate success. When you set your heart to chasing a goal, your chances of success will multiply. Think about that new car you bought or the trip you went on last year. What about the first house you bought? Did you have your heart set on it? Notice that I said "heart", not "mind". Heartset is emotional. Mindset is logical. Emotional decisions usually win out in the end.

NOTE: We will discuss Heartset and Mindset in greater depth in Key Number 5.

For some people the idea can be as simple as deciding to study for a new career. For others it may be to change jobs or start a small business from home.

Changing Careers –

Just because you are a Bookkeeper doesn't mean you need to study to be an Accountant. They are two similar, but different, professions. As a hairdresser, do you really need to be a beautician as well? Search deep inside yourself. What occupation inspires you?

Perhaps you're a plumber who is a very active sportsman (or sports woman). You may consider a career change by becoming a

Personal Trainer. Or, you may utilise your computer skills by becoming an IT specialist.

Whatever you decide, spend as much time as you can on thinking about "how it will make you feel".

Going Into Business –

Most people who go into business on a part time basis do not have a bottomless pit of ready money. They usually decide to take the safe option by starting their home based business, often with less than $1,000 in capital. Whilst this can work very well for some, many find that it is no more than a hobby because of the lack of time they can spare to kick the business off.

Still, many businesses start out as a hobby (eg. Craft, web designers, artists, internet marketers, second hand dealers, eBay sellers, party planners, authors, furniture makers, leather goods manufacturers, dance teachers etc).

A large percentage of people start out part time and quit their job when it becomes apparent that they can make a living out of doing something that they love. Personally, this is the model I prefer as long as you choose something you love... something you must do... something that you look forward to, even if it means working well into the night or on weekends.

Ask yourself, "How do I feel when I work on my business? Does it inspire me? Do I feel like I am achieving something worthwhile? Am I creating the lifestyle I enjoy?"

Those who decide to start their own business usually do so because they don't like working for someone else (eg. Plumbers, electricians, hairdressers, bookkeepers, lawyers, doctors, accountants, cleaners, IT consultants, web designers etc).

Some people just need a change of career or a *"sea change".* You may be bored with your job, looking for a new challenge or you may have identified an opportunity that suits your skills.

Whatever your situation, you need to consider:

- What you want to do

- Why you want to do it

- How will it make you feel

- Is this business something that you really want to do? Ask yourself *"Why is it important to me?"* You **must** be able to answer this question. Does it excite you? If not, why not? Is it likely to be driving you on 12 months from now?

Important Point: You simply must love what you do or it won't last. Choose your future wisely.

I cannot stress how important that this point is. It is the glue that will hold you and your future success together when times get tough. And there will always be some tough times mixed in with all the good times. That, along with death and taxes, is the one thing that is guaranteed in life.

I'm sure that you will agree that it is better to work at what you love, rather than work at a job you hate.

"Why?"

This simple three letter word is critical when planning your future.

If you don't have a strong enough *"Why"*, your chances of long term success can reduce dramatically. What will drive you to succeed in your career or your own business? What will get you out of bed each day with a spring in your step? Is it the lifestyle, the money, the self-satisfaction, the time spent with the family, time to pursue sporting interests, service to the community, volunteering, fighting for a cause, the opportunity to change the world, the unique and useful product or service you offer?

Remember that it may feel right for you today, **but how will you feel** about it in 12 months' time? What about 2 years from now? Is it a career business move that can sustain you for 5 years or more?

Remember This: You must know your reason for doing something before you even think about how you will do it. Asking yourself "What" and "Why" must always come before you ask "How".

2. RESEARCHING THE IDEA AND THE MARKET

The internet is a wonderful business tool when used to its full potential. We can access everything from Government statistics to articles, blogs, videos, social media, forums and websites on specialist subjects.

Government sites from around the globe have a Statistics Department where you can learn an enormous amount of detail about your chosen career, business or potential market.

Demographics can tell you a lot about local and international markets. You can find out where your potential employers are based or where your targeted customers live, their age, marital status, occupation, income, children etc.

Facebook, Twitter, LinkedIn and YouTube can help you to communicate and engage with your prospective markets. If you are planning to start a business, begin by asking your Facebook and Twitter friends what they think of your business idea.

Set up an online Survey and ask 4 or 5 relevant questions about your business. This is a great way to find out if you may be onto a winner. Ask your friends to send the Survey on to their friends.

NOTE: Don't forget to specify a time for completion and return of the survey.

International and local Business networking groups will help you to connect with business people all around the world. Local Business Chambers and Business Enterprise Centres are also very helpful when doing your research.

In particular, LinkedIn is a great platform for Professionals and Business people to connect. Linking and connecting with influential people in industries and occupations you would like to enter can really pay off in a big way if you persist and learn how this platform works.

3.   CREATING A PERSONAL ACTION PLAN

Regardless of whether you are aiming to change careers, get a new job of start a new business, you need a Plan. Most business owners have a Business Plan. But, how many wage earners have ever sat down and written out a Personal Action Plan? How many of you have ever heard of a Personal Action Plan? Not many, I'm guessing!

A Personal Plan, or Business Plan, can be as long or as short as necessary for your particular career aspirations or your business idea. Many Financial Companies such as banks have Business Plan templates on their websites.

As for Personal Action Plans, you can create your own on a Word Document. Don't forget to include a budget so you are well aware of how much you need to earn to enable you to live comfortably.

A good Plan, whether it be Personal or Business, needs to have **a Vision, a Mission Statement, Goals, Objectives, a Budget and an Action Plan.** Without these 6 features it is a Wish, not a Plan.

So, how important is a Personal or Business Plan?

A Business Plan is vital to forecast the path of your business. It helps to determine if you have a financially viable business idea. So, it makes complete sense that if you have a Personal Action Plan it will also help you to keep track of your results, and to see if you are on target to achieve your goals.

If you wish to borrow money to set up or to expand the business, your Bank Manager will ask to see your Business Plan. Imagine how impressed he/she would be if you showed him/her your Personal Action Plan when applying to borrow money for a new car or your first home. I bet they would never have seen a Personal Action Plan.

As a Small Business Trainer and Mentor, when doing my Business Plan, I found that it helped me to focus on costs, pricing and profit margins. It also assisted in deciding what products and services that my potential customers wanted or needed. For me, value was critical so I chose to over-deliver good value products and services wherever possible.

My Plan also helped me to forecast potential problems and down time. This ensured that in the event of sickness or injury, I could survive for substantial periods of time. It also allowed for flexibility and rapid changes of direction where needed.

This planning, as it turned out, was invaluable. At the time of writing this book (September/October 2016), I am battling Cancer, and have been since early this year. Like many life threatening diseases, Cancer snuck up on me with little or no warning.

Chemotherapy, radiotherapy and a major operation was unplanned and meant that I could no longer train or mentor my clients.

Writing, however, has kept me active and enabled me to make a living online. Life goes on if you are prepared to be flexible.

Had I not taken the time to do a Business Plan and a Personal Action Plan I may have missed these highly important points.

Important Point.....

A written Plan works because **it makes you focus on what you really want.** And, in business, it also makes you focus on what your customers really want so they will keep buying from you. It's as simple as that!

THE SECOND KEY
MODERN MARKETING

1.   MARKETING IN THE 21ST CENTURY

Marketing YOU

How do you present yourself to a future Employer or Customer?

Do you look the part? Do you dress to suit your career, profession and status in the community? How do you conduct yourself in front of Customers and peers? Do you interview well when applying for a job? Can you write a compelling CV?

What skills and qualifications do you possess? **Can you "sell" yourself?** What experience do you have? Do you come across as being knowledgeable about your business, products or chosen occupation? Do you come with outstanding referrals from highly credible people you have worked with?

Regardless of whether you are applying for a job or a promotion, or maybe you are consulting with a Client or Customer, you need to know what you are talking about. You need to be able to tell great stories, ask questions, show interest and produce valid suggestions.

Above all, you need to be likeable, friendly and positive. Marketing yourself affectively is just so important these days.

Marketing A Business

Unless you own a retail store, a hotel or a food shop with good passing traffic, you may have some measure of difficulty attracting customers when you get started in business. Even those who have been in business for many years can experience the occasional trough when nothing much appears to be happening. These can be worrying times and some extra planning needs to be done to reduce or eliminate these periods of low productivity.

It is during these times of low buyer activity that many businesses *"fall over"*.

Along with poor management and business skills, lack of marketing and networking skills are major causes of small business failure.

Throwing money at an Advertising Campaign is often thought, by business owners, to be the **"silver bullet"** that will fix the problem. Often the result is a disaster for the cash strapped business. The credit card takes a beating and you're on your way to another meeting with the Bank Manager to extend the overdraft or refinance the line of credit.

The smart business owner does not just blindly advertise in Yellow Pages or grab a half page ad in the local paper. They don't run endless radio and TV campaigns that just break even.

The smart business owner measures the results and drops the under-performing ads. The smart business owner knows which advertising is working and directs resources to the most profitable campaigns.

Get Known

In addition he, or she, builds relationships with their customers. They collect email addresses and send newsletters and catalogues to their customers. They ask their customers to send their friends to the store or they ask for direct referrals.

They meet regularly with other business owners for coffee and they attend business networking events. They keep up to date on the latest trends in their industry; they welcome new ideas and continue to learn new business skills and marketing techniques. They involve themselves in the community.

The secret is that there is no secret. These business owners are savvy people. They understand the power of being known in the community as a trusted authority in their chosen field. They go out of their way to become well known, friendly and helpful.

And now, as we move further into the 21st Century, business owners are using the power of the Internet to connect with people they could never previously reach.

The rise...and rise...and rise of Social Media Marketing means that you can now leverage the Internet like never before. You can extend the reach of your business to the next town, the next city, the next state and around the globe if you so desire. You can now compete on the same stage as mega corporations such as McDonalds, Coca Cola and Dell Computers.

Right now, for the small business owner, the world is yours like never before. For a fraction of traditional advertising costs, you can reach a totally new global market. If you are still stuck using the outdated sales and marketing methods of the 80s and 90s, it's time to get out of the 20th Century and start using the technology that's available to us all right now.

Advertising

At this point, it's probably a good idea to stop and think about where your advertising dollar is going. Are you still blowing the budget on Yellow Pages and newspaper ads? Are they working like they used to? Are you making less money now than you used to? If the answer is **"Yes"**, it's time to make the change.

If you aren't prepared to step out of last century, you will not be ready for what comes next in this Book. **I am about to introduce**

you to what will be, for some, a totally new way of doing business.

Building relationships with your customers, giving great service, networking with other business people, using Social Media sites such as YouTube, Facebook, Twitter and LinkedIn, learning to engage with your potential customers, having fun.....this is what works today.

The old sales and marketing tricks are D.E.A.D. my friends. We live in a rapidly changing world. Whether we like it or not, social selling has landed.....and it's not going away any time soon.

2. BUILDING RELATIONSHIPS

In the 1980s a very dangerous trend emerged in business. The **"Greed is Good Philosophy"** as made famous by Gordon Gekko in the movie, **"Wall Street"**, took hold in real life.

Many sales people, especially those involved in selling insurance, finance, investment, second hand cars and property **"bent the truth"** or just blatantly told lies to get the sale. They made outrageous guarantees they couldn't keep, they hid important facts, they were encouraged by ruthless sales managers to stretch the truth and many got very rich.

In the 80s, sales people were taught to start closing the Sale at the first opportunity. No need to list all the benefits. **Just "sign them up"** and move on to the next sucker. Most people don't fall for those tricks these days. They are much better informed and educated.

When the Share Market crashed in October 1987, the house of cards came down. When the property markets went south a couple of years later, things really started to change. Governments, banks and finance companies cracked down on unscrupulous selling tactics.

Since then, the sales industry has undergone a complete makeover. Governments put extra regulations in place that "protected" the Buyer. And, with the help of the Internet, we can now make informed decisions about companies, products and people.

These days it does not take long to identify shonky sales and business people. Once something bad, or really good, gets posted on Facebook or Twitter, it can go viral in a matter of hours.....which brings me to **building relationships.**

It is not difficult to build good relationships with customers or clients. It works like this. The potential customer has the money. You would like them to give you some of that money. So, how do you get it?

Simple....try putting yourself in their shoes. If you were the potential customer, what would you want them to do for you?

Example:

You are going out for dinner. You find 2 restaurants side by side. Both restaurants sell your favourite food except one is more expensive than the other. You look inside Restaurant Number 1 (the cheaper restaurant) and it is chaotic. Waiters are running everywhere and looking frustrated, the noise coming from the kitchen is disconcerting and the diners don't look happy.

Inside Restaurant Number 2 (the more expensive restaurant) the place is packed, the mood is upbeat, the waiters have smiles on their faces and the diners look like they're having fun. Which one would you choose?

Most people would pick Restaurant Number 2 because it has what they want.....good food, a system and a happy atmosphere. This restaurant understands that building rapport with the customers pays dividends.

Restaurant Number 1 dipped out because they gave the impression that they did not know what to do. Nor did they care. Chaos generally means that the business has managers with no people skills, poor staff and no systems.

3. LEVERAGING: NETWORKING AND REFERRAL MARKETING

Networking is underutilised by many professionals and small business owners. Mixing with other people in business, sharing ideas and learning about each other's businesses will get you known in the community and seen as an expert in your field.

It will also get you plenty of new business as people start to refer their friends, family and clients to you. This rarely happens immediately but as other business people and customers learn to trust you, they are only too happy to tell others what a great job you did for them.

Regular attendance at local Business Networking Events will also lift your profile in the business community. The more events you attend and the more business owners you meet, the more recognisable you become. This leads to familiarity and you become known as a local authority in your field.

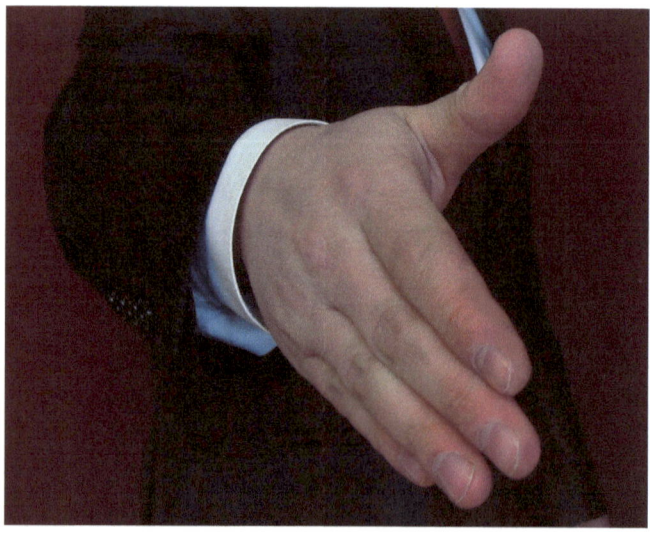

Check out your local clubs, Business Chambers, Networking Groups, Rotary, Lions and Small Business Clubs etc. Get involved with charitable events and be seen and known in your Community.

Friends, family, customers and clients are a great source of referrals. Tell them that your best business comes from referrals. Ask them if they would be willing to give you a written testimonial that you can put on your website or post on Facebook. Referrals cost nothing but they can create massive professional and business growth.

4.   SOCIAL MEDIA MARKETING

A few years ago Social Media Marketing was little more than a blip on the radar. The idea of promoting anything via Facebook was virtually unheard of. Social Media was for people to share family photos, catch up with friends and stay in touch with people overseas.

The Obama presidential campaign helped to change all that. In February 2007 Barack Obama met with a Facebook board member to discuss the possibility of conducting a political campaign through Social Media. The rest is history and many of the world's largest companies sat up and took notice.

Within a few short years names like McDonalds, Coca Cola and Dell had huge Social Media presences. Singers, musicians and sports stars now have hundreds of millions of followers on Twitter. LinkedIn is the place to be for business and professional people.

These days, all sorts of careers are launched on YouTube. Professionals are head hunted on LinkedIn and Local Small Business has found Facebook in a big, big way. Pinterest and Instagram have also become big names recently.

It's getting hard to keep up.

Social Media has changed and the small business market has caught on. This is no longer a trend. Social Media has become the way to get your business message, your brand and your personal profile out there.

Facebook assists people to run targeted ads. If you want to sell jewellery to 20 – 30 year old women who have recently become engaged within a 50km radius of your shop, you can target these women. If you just want to create a profile for you or your business, LinkedIn, Facebook, Twitter and YouTube are ideal.

Social Media Marketing may be relatively new but it is now the Number One Game in town. If you are not yet in the game, make the decision to get into it **NOW!**

5. UP SELLING AND CROSS SELLING

When a customer enters your computer shop and asks for your advice on a new laptop, do you ask questions?

I hope so, because ***"Questions Are The Answer"*** says world renowned Body Language expert, Alan Pease. Do you just offer the customer the latest computer or do you compare two or three brands to help the customer reach the right decision?

Do you ask what the computer will be used for? Is it for you or the kids? Will it be used for home computing, study, playing games or will it be used primarily for business? Are you helping the customer make a good decision or are you just a product peddler?

Do you offer Virus protection or accessories such as a laptop bag? Do you suggest an extended warranty to your customer? If not, you could be leaving thousands of dollars on the table.

THE THIRD KEY
EXECUTION AND IMPLEMENTATION

The Idea is where it all begins. Research will tell you if your Idea is feasible. Marketing lets people know that you exist. Now it's time to go to work.

Creating Systems Is Vital To Success In Business Or Career

As an Employee, it is a requirement that you follow the systems put in place by Management. But, you can create your own systems that will streamline your work.

For instance, do you arrive early at work to set up your Workplace? Do you create a Daily List of tasks to complete? Do you schedule meetings and arrive on time? Do you prepare for appointments and interviews? Do you remember to take short breaks away from your computer? Do you spend 15 minutes a day thinking about what needs to be done tomorrow? Do you take time out to relax after the workday is finished?

All of these things will create an effective system you can use at work regardless of whether you are a Manager, Business Owner or Staff Member.

If you are an Owner or Manager who has staff, they should all be familiar with the systems you have implemented. If you have a chicken shop you need to have an ordering system that ensures that you have a fresh supply of chickens daily.

You must not run out of fresh milk, bread, buns and salad. Each individual must know his or her job. Staff must be able to cover for each other in the case of an emergency.

Just think of the system that McDonalds employs where 15 year old kids run the store. Your system must be that effective and that simple.

If you're a Sole Trader, how do you continue to operate when you are sick? Having systems in place will allow you to hire people on a temporary basis. A basic manual or set of instructions is all it takes. No systems means that you will have to shut the business down until you recover.

Build quality into your systems.

Quality builds reliability and enables you to gain a reputation as someone that people can trust. Treating your staff, peers and customers as important people will work all the time.

Think of what makes you go back to a shop time and time again.....a smile, a friendly voice and a helpful nature. Often, that is all it takes.

No matter what role you play at your day to day job/profession, remember that if you show that you are there to help and to solve problems, those who matter will seek you out as the Expert. You will stand out from the crowd and be rewarded for your efforts.

Example:

If my toaster broke and I needed a new one, what I want to know is *"what is the best toaster in the shop that suits my needs"*. If I live alone, I may only need a toaster that browns two slices of toast at a time. If I have 4 teenagers at home, I will probably need a much bigger toaster.

Quality service means asking questions that help the customer make the right decision. Quality products that do the job that the consumer wants coupled with quality service that makes the customer feel happy with their purchase will guarantee that your customer is not lost to the competition.

Bad service and a pushy salesperson means "Buyer's Remorse". This can mean dissatisfaction in the product, the price, the staff, the shop, the management and often means a product return and a refund the next day.

Always ensure that the Customer leaves with a smile on their dial and a reason to return to buy again and again.

Pricing

"So, what about price?" you say.

It is true that many of us buy on price. However, poor service and low quality products can never make up for true quality.

There are thousands of examples of higher priced items dominating the market over lower priced items because of quality. Why do men buy $1,000 Italian suits? Why do women spend a fortune on makeovers? Why would people choose to spend a year's wages on a cruise on the Queen Mary II when they can choose a much cheaper cruise, or series of cruises?

Quality! That's why. The Queen Mary II is recognised as the ultimate in cruising. People pay a whole heap more for quality, and they will rave about it to all of their friends for years.

Important Points....

Only quality products and quality service will earn you the right to charge higher prices. The moral of the story is this....if you have a product that sells for $50 and you want to sell it for $100, focus on quality in everything you do. Always give more than the customer expects and it's only a matter of time before you can charge premium prices for your goods and services.

Quality work by a Quality Employee will be rewarded in time.

Outsourcing – A Favourite Subject Of Mine

Outsourcing is not just for the Big Guys anymore and smaller businesses are turning to Outsourcers in countries such as The Philippines, India, Sri Lanka, Pakistan and Bangladesh to get casual work done.

Specialised jobs such as Web Design, Search Engine Optimisation, article writing, blogging, promotional video production and Social Media marketing are available at a fraction of the price you will pay to hire people in Australia, New Zealand, USA, England and Canada.

I use Filipino Virtual Assistants to help me with Facebook, Twitter, YouTube, websites and design of Book Covers. I prefer to write my own content but pass on the work that I'm not so good at to a team of VAs.

Having Virtual Assistants allows me to focus on the work I am good at and plan for the future. **And, I have found that Filipinos are fantastic workers!**

I can write, market, sell, teach, mentor and consult... but I am not a designer and I am not young enough to be an internet guru. So, I pay the people who can do what I can't or don't like doing. I'd much prefer to be writing, marketing, networking or selling. Why do stuff you don't like doing when you can do what you love?

Even Employees Can Have A Virtual Assistant

This may be a new concept to you, but it make sense to pay someone $5 - $10 USD per hour to help you with a few hours of web design or research than doing something that is not in your area of specialisation. It might also just save you a headache or two, as well.

Why Filipinos?

I tried Outsourcers from other Asian countries but found that it is easier to deal with Filipinos. There are fewer language problems, they work hard, they are keen to please and they are always coming up with great ideas.

That is not to say that you can't get quality workers from India, for instance. It's just that I was looking for assistants that I could communicate with and were close to my time zone.

I have found that the Filipino VAs work is first class.....and, they come at a very affordable price. My Virtual Assistants treat my business as though it was their own and they are always eager to please. I often wonder how I did without them!

THE FOURTH KEY
INNOVATION

The foundation of any Personal, Business or Professional Success is innovation.

You need a Unique Selling Proposition (USP)

Who you are or what your product or service is about needs to be different. However, once you have that competitive edge, it can be very difficult to maintain at times.

Innovation is all about looking forward to predict the future. What's coming next? Will you be at the forefront of Change?

Where will I be next year? Where will my business be in 5 years' time? What are the market trends? Do I need to reset my course to compete in the future? What about changes in personal and family circumstances?

If business is good and your personal situation is on an even keel, it can become a little too easy to shut out these questions.

The main source of innovation will often come directly from employees. They know their job very well. Therefore, innovation will often come naturally to them and you should be actively encouraging them to try new ways of doing things.

Young people, in particular, embrace Change so they should be consulted when major innovation is planned... the older generation tend to reject changes in their workplace. They prefer to preserve the status quo.

But, what if **YOU** are the business? What if you are out there alone, trying to perform all functions of the business such as manufacturing, marketing, advertising, sales, planning, forecasting and record keeping?

If you are a business owner with no staff, innovation can only come from you. Don't become complacent. Constantly stretch yourself with new ideas. Stay up to date with new trends in your industry. Continue to educate yourself. Your profession demands it.

Innovation is important to keep your career or business moving in the right direction. In these difficult economic times it can become a matter of survival.

You must take time out from to identify areas that can be improved or done differently. Part of this innovation process may be to enrol in a Course or hire a Virtual Assistant.

Innovative solutions can not only solve business problems but they must also **align with your personal goals as well as the goals of your staff and your clients.**

Innovation can define the culture of your workplace and enhance your reputation in the community. Don't ignore it.

Important Point....

In a recent Blog by Flagpole Software (www.flagpole-software.com) they explained the importance of innovation in a very succinct manner –

"There's no lack of opportunities for businesses to 'create' -- creating new products or service offerings, creating new markets to pursue, creating new advertising, and so on. But 'creation' doesn't always mean you're innovating. The difference between creating and true business innovation is that the latter involves taking a serious, hard look at the needs of your customers and doing only that which you know will change the game for them and for your business."

To sum it all up, constant innovation shows that you are a forward thinker who is interested in the needs of Management, Staff and Customers....not just the bottom line. Innovation where your customers and staff win means that you win.

Just look at companies like Apple, Microsoft, Virgin, Nike, Twitter, Facebook, ALDI, LinkedIn, Google etc. These companies are constantly innovating and regularly make the list of Top 100 Innovative Companies as well as being amongst the Top Income Earners. And that is the value of innovation!

Important Point....

The philosophy of every one of these companies is to give the buyer exactly what they want, when they want it. Nothing else matters. They realise that if they put the customer's needs first, then the money will follow.

THE FIFTH KEY
MINDSET VS HEARTSET

What About The "Winner's Mindset?"

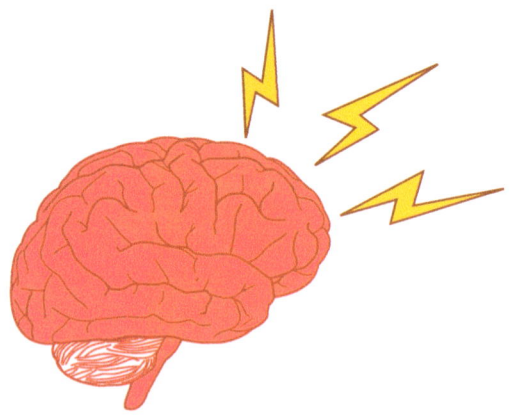

The Winner's Mindset is a combination of many things but it can be broken into four basic elements - Belief System, Will Power, Positive Outlook and Gut Feeling.

- Belief System. The Winner believes that they are providing a great service and that their business is economically important to the community. They project this belief in themselves in a confident, knowledgeable and friendly manner.

- **Will Power.** Winners make decisions. When the decisions are made, will power carries them through the tough times....and there will be some tough times.

- **Positive Outlook.** If you have done your planning and have a strong belief in yourself and your decisions, you will project a confident image. You will approach each day with certainty and nothing will shake your resolve. A positive outlook is a trait that all Winners share.

- **Gut Feeling.** Winners often make decisions based on Gut Feeling. Whilst there appears to be no logical or scientific reason for this, Gut Feeling is a very powerful Decision making tool. A gut feeling usually has its roots in experience. Winners will often make snap decisions simply because it either **"feels right"** or **"it just didn't seem right at the time"**.

Mindset is often the forgotten ingredient in business and personal life. **Or is it?**

"Having the correct mindset will eventually determine your ultimate success". I'm sure that you have all heard that before.

But, is it true? Some of us say, *"Not necessarily".* And there's a very good reason that we dispute this.

Because, as Dr Robert Anthony states in his excellent video series titled *"The Secret of Deliberate Creation",* you are less likely to follow through on goals that are set by the mind rather than those goals that are determined by the heart.

Think about this for a moment. You've just seen the house of your dreams. You have to have it and it's in your price range. You will move heaven and earth to get that house. What is driving you right now? It's definitely your heart... not your mind.

We've all heard the saying, **"She had her heart set on getting that job"** or **"He put his heart and soul into building that business"**. Heartset usually wins out over Mindset. Why is that, do you think?

So, why does Heartset win out?

Simple... because it is emotional and linked to your Life Purpose.

Mindset is logical and takes effort to keep re-focusing on the ultimate goal. This is why Key Performance Indicators (KPIs) are rarely achieved in the workplace. KPIs are simply goals set by management that Employees often don't buy into because they fail to have an emotional attachment.

KPI's are driven by a need for more productivity in the workplace. Often, a 10% increase in productivity is linked to Team Performance and is rewarded by a 2% pay rise for all. This rarely works because Employees can see through this. A far better option is a collaborative approach that rewards individuals for outstanding performance.

Example One:

Susan is an Inbound Sales Consultant who sets her Quarterly Sales Targets with the help of her Supervisor. She then exceeds her sales goals by 10% for the Quarter. Susan then earns a cash bonus of $5,000. Susan has bought into workplace goals because she sees what's in it for her.

Example Two:

Jenny, and her workmates, are required by Management to exceed their previous targets by 10%. For that, she will receive a pay increase of 2% as long as "the team" also perform to the required level.

Assuming that Susan and Jenny were earning a Base Salary of $60,000 per year, who would you rather be... Susan or Jenny? KPIs, unfortunately, rarely work because only a handful of Employees are capable of hitting preset targets.

It is also true that a percentage of Employees have no ambition to over-achieve and are happy with their base rate of pay. Others have outside priorities and can't commit to targets due to family and social commitments.

Your Heart's Desire

Emotional goals have a far greater chance of success than logical goals.

Knowing exactly what you want out of your career or business life is essential to professional and personal satisfaction. Your Personal

Action Plan needs input from the heart. It is your ***heart's desire*** that guides you, not your mindset.

Don't get me wrong. Mindset does play a part in your overall success. But, having a Winner's Mindset is one thing. Having your heart set on an outcome is another. Only your true heart's desire will ensure that you follow through on your plans, goals and aspirations. Trusting your heart will lead you along the path that can give you lasting happiness, enjoyment and personal satisfaction.

Mindset is temporary. Your True Heart's Desire is lasting. It brings you back on track when all is falling down around you. It is the glue that allows you to get back up after being knocked down. It is that Inner Voice that says, **"This setback will not stop me. I am on a mission."**

OK. So, What Is Your True Heart's Desire?

Your Heart's Desire is not easy to determine. It takes time, energy, thought and a genuine attempt to look deep inside yourself to uncover your True Heart's Desire.

It's not some 30 second decision, fad, hope or whim. It's all about who you are and how it makes you feel. It's your inner being shouting out loud that this is what you truly want.

Your Heart's Desire will be a 100 out of 100 on your scale of Wants and Must Haves. It won't be 80/100 or even 90/100. It will measure 100 on your scale and you'll know when you find it.

Just remember, it's unlikely that you'll find your True Heart's Desire at your first attempt. You must be diligent. Don't stop searching until you find it. You will be glad that you took the time to only accept Number 1 on your "Must Have Scale".

I cannot stress just how important that this step is if you really want to discover your Life Purpose and have a truly successful life.

The Fifth Key? Or the First Key?

The Heartset that you adopt in your life is so important that _it should actually be the First Key_ to success. Nine times out of ten the Heartset that you take into your business and personal life will be the difference between having fun, making new friends, attracting success, becoming financially free or experiencing total and utter frustration.

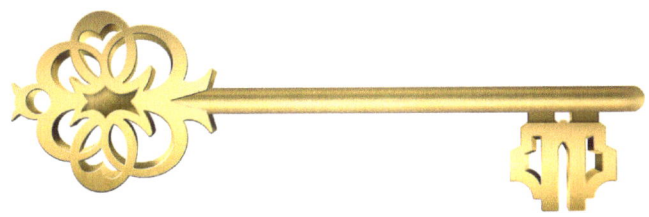

So, what do I mean by this?

Consider the following example:

Jack and Ben are both very experienced and competent Electricians who decide to start their own businesses on the same day in a town of 250,000 people. They have done their research and have determined that the market is large enough for both of them to get plenty of work.

However, 6 months later, Jack is complaining that Ben is getting twice as much work as him. They both advertise extensively and they have the same skills. So, why is Ben getting all the work? Jack is becoming increasingly frustrated about this state of affairs. Some of his customers have even dropped him and got Ben to do their work. Jack just can't understand it.

On the other hand, Ben is having a great time. He networks regularly with other business people, he is always busy and his customers love him. They are always telling their friends about the great job he does and how he is always on time.

Other tradesmen send him referrals. In fact, he is getting so much work that he is now thinking of asking Jack to help him out during the busy times. The only problem is that Jack is always complaining these days. Ben feels that he cannot take the risk with Jack. He doesn't want to lose customers.

The only real difference between Ben and Jack is that Ben understands the difference between Mindset and Heartset. He has positive thoughts and takes action. He loves his work and it shows. Ben's customers love him because he is competent, punctual, happy, and friendly...and he has a positive outlook.

He is a person that people can like and he believes in himself. Ben has taken the time to set goals that are aligned to his heart rather than his mind. He attracts customers and friends.

Jack, on the other hand, has low self-esteem, thinks that his customers slow him down with their dumb questions and can't understand why he is so unlucky. He is jealous of Ben because he gets all the work.

THE SUMMARY

Successful people are Realists. They know what they want and they understand that they are only in demand if they offer quality work or a valued service.

Successful business owners and professionals also know that they will stay in business for as long as they receive a great Customer Experience. In this day and age it is absolutely critical to follow business trends.

Things have just moved so quickly in the first few years of the 21st Century. Just think about it.....High Definition Smart TVs, iPhones, iPads, Bluetooth, solar towers, driverless cars, virtual keyboards, hybrid cars, birth control patches, YouTube, Facebook, LinkedIn, Twitter and Google. None of these were around in the Year 2000.

What next? One thing is for certain. Technology will continue to change our lives into the future. When Social Media can change politics like it has in the USA and Egypt a few years ago, just imagine where we will be over the next 10 years.

I sat in on a Webinar recently where one of the Speakers suggested that 60% of the jobs that people will be performing over the next 6 or 7 years haven't been invented yet. Technology and Medicine are taking giant strides. Driverless cars are already here as are smart watches. And what about 3D printers? I still can't wrap my head around that one.

The Final Message

Look at the new careers that are popping up on a daily basis. How many new businesses and new jobs will be around in 2025?

Are you ready for the Future? Will you survive if we have another Global Financial Crisis? It's time to prepare. Do not wait for life to change around you. Change with it. We live in interesting and exciting times. Prepare to compete....and WIN!

I hope that this Book has helped. Why not join me on Facebook for more insights?

All the best for your present and your future.

John Kirk

Author, Speaker and Trainer

Email: johnkirkonline@gmail.com
www.facebook.com/JohnKirkSBA

ABOUT THE AUTHOR - JOHN KIRK

For more than 45 years John worked in both the Public and Private Sectors as well as being self-employed for more than 20 years. During the 1970's and through to the early 1980's he worked as a Systems Auditor for the Australian Department of Defence.

From 1982 to 1984 John held a management position with a large American Finance Company before leaving to set up his own Insurance Agency and Financial Consultancy. Between 1985 and 2003, John serviced many hundreds of clients and trained nearly 150 salespeople and customer service staff.

In 2003 he joined the Australian Taxation Office as a GST Field Auditor and Small Business Educator where his role was to assist the small business person to keep better records and comply with Tax laws.

Retiring from the ATO in September 2010, John is now a Small Business Trainer and Mentor, Speaker, Author and committed Business Networker. He is an advocate of Small Business. His clients include individuals and start-up businesses as well as established business owners.